Vision Planner

Stephanie R. Burns

College Edition

♪estiny
Entertainment Kenner, LA

Cover Design – Stephanie R Burns, Destiny Marketing Group

Photograph - © Aramanda/Fotolio.com

Copy Editors – Susan Gebhardt and Monica Chambers

Vision Planner and The Business of My Art™ series can be purchased for educational, business, or sales promotional use. For more information, please write The Business of My Art c/o Destiny Entertainment, PO Box 640448, Kenner, LA 70064

www.TheBusinessOfMyArt.com

Destiny Entertainment, LLC

PO Box 640448

Kenner, LA 70064

www.Destinyentertain.com

All definitions taken from Encarta Dictionary

Introduction

How important is it to have a vision? The Bible says that without it, the people perish. Perish?! According to Encarta, that means to be "non-existing". That's a powerful statement; without a vision, we are non-existing. I can be a little stressed at times, but it wasn't until I lost focus on my vision that I became really ill. That's right…I became sick. I had no idea that an unclear vision creates stress, stress…sickness and sickness that if not treated, could eventually lead to death. (*This is what it truly means to be non-existing.*)

Just imagine yourself in school studying to become an artist, an entrepreneur, or your choice of your dreams. Finals are coming up, you are working two jobs to make ends meet, you have a family to take care of, and it suddenly becomes too overwhelming. You forget why you came to school, and you want to give up. That's because you're focusing more on the *stress* than on your actual **vision** and goals.

I created this planner *just for you*. When you write down your vision and goals, you are then reminded why you are doing what you are doing. The stress becomes more manageable, and you realize that this too shall pass.

It's okay if you do not have a vision yet. This planner will guide you in discovering and unlocking your vision and provide tools to keep you on track. It will be your guide in establishing goals, building a networking plan, tracking lessons learned, and accomplishments earned. I wish above all for you to walk in purpose and destiny. Be blessed!

Stephanie R. Burns

Getting Started

In order to get the best out of this planner, I have provided the layout and a few tips on how to use it.

This monthly planner covers four years…your time in college. However, it is okay if you do not get started until your junior/senior year or if your program has fewer than four years. The point is to get started.

Quotes: There are monthly quotes to keep you motivated and charged.

Month/Year: Since this planner starts when you do, there is no set date. You will just fill in the month and year as you go.

Vision: Your vision is simply **what you want to become**…your purpose and destiny. Some people know exactly what they want to do, and others do not have a clue. It's okay if in the first year you haven't figured it out yet. That is what going to college is all about. Here are few tips to help you unlock your vision:

- Year 1 – **Getting started**. Think about things you like. Write down your major and why you chose it.

- Year 2 – **Moving ahead.** For year two, modify your vision. Have you changed majors? Have you found a new passion?

- Year 3 – **Clarity.** This year, your vision should start to come in focus. What do you expect in year four? How does your vision support your expectations?

- Year 4 – **Ability to see.** By year four, you should have defined your vision and are ready to act on it. If you are still having trouble with your vision, start over again.

Goals: Define goals that will help you support your vision. If you do not have a vision yet, use this section to record any goals you have for the month. It could be something as simple as finding a job.

Your goals should be:

- Measurable
- Realistic
- Attainable

Date Achieved: It's important that you measure your progress. Date achieved section is included for you to track the point when you were able to accomplish your goals. Even if it takes you a year to achieve it, make sure to go back and fill in the date.

The People I've Met: Networking is very important in achieving your goals and fulfilling your destiny. You are not here to do things alone. Make it a goal to meet 1 to 5 new people every month. While doing so, make sure that you follow-up with them on a regular basis.

Networking Type: Networking contacts are categorized into five types: Supporters, Partners, Connectors, Mentors, and Learners. Make sure to track this category when you do meet someone. *Note: Your networking contact can fall in several categories types e.g., a person can be your supporter and your mentor.*

1. **Supporters** – Supporters are the people who will motivate and encourage you.

2. **Partners** – These are the people who have similar goals as yours.

3. **Connectors** – Connectors are very instrumental as they will help you achieve your goals or connect you to those who can.

4. **Mentors** – Mentors and leaders are people who will teach you or provide you with life lessons.

5. **Learners** – These are people that **you** will help achieve *their* goals.

Notes/Lessons Learned: This section is where you can write any notes about the lessons you've learned this month, any items you may have researched, ideas, and thoughts you may have.

Graphic Symbols: There are three graphic symbols that will require some action from you.

Stop	Expects you to stop before proceeding.
Yield	Provides tips or cautions you to slow down.
Go	Permits you to proceed; you are on track!

Example: Here is an example to follow.

"Where there is no vision, the people perish" — *The Bible (KJV)*

Month *01*   Year *200x*

My Vision:

I like working with young adults so I decided to major in education.

My vision is to become a teacher. I also enjoy singing.

My Monthly Goals	Date Achieved
1. To get an A in class	3/21
2. Talk to two instructors about the advantages and disadvantages of teaching.	1/25
3. Sign-up for the Big Brother/Big Sister program.	3/01

People I've Met	Networking Type *(Supporter, Partner, Connector, Mentor, Learner)*
1. Jane Masters	**Mentor**
2. Doris Day	**Supporter**
3. John Davis	**Learner, Partner**

Notes/Lessons learned:

I researched the Big Brother/Big Sister programs in the area. Took two months to complete. Met Jane Masters my English teacher. She gave me insight on teaching and other organizations to join. Doris Day is my roommate and she's more excited about me becoming a teacher than I think I am☺. John is one of the young men that I am mentoring who also wants to be a singer one day. One of my classes was pretty hard, but Jane Masters tutored me. I am still very excited about becoming a teacher and I still enjoy singing.

Year 1

Vision (noun) – *the ability to see.* Having a vision is simply the ability to see yourself in the future. To know your purpose and destiny.

Why are you here? It is more than just to take up space. Coming to college is a step in the right direction. College is the place where we come to "find ourselves"…to really see what we want to do and what we don't want to do. Forget about homework and your teachers for a second…what is that burning desire inside of you? What are you passionate about?

You may find that this is the year of transition and survival, of transitioning into a new place and learning to survive in a new place.

As you go through this year, focus on yourself. Learn to make yourself a priority and don't let anyone steer you off track. Take mental notes about your behavior. Is there a class you can't wait to attend? Have you found a hobby you really like? What types of people interest you?

It's okay if you haven't found your vision yet. Start by writing your major and why you chose this major. The key is to be honest with yourself.

If you have a major, likes or dislikes, and / or you have a glimpse of your vision, you are ready to get started!

"Where there is no vision, the people perish." — The Bible (KJV)

Month _____   Year _____

My Vision:

_____

_____

_____

_____

_____

_____

My Monthly Goals	Date Achieved
1.	
2.	
3.	
4.	
5.	

People I've Met	Networking Type *(Supporter, Partner, Connector, Mentor, Learner)*
1.	
2.	
3.	
4.	
5.	

Notes/Lessons Learned:

"As long as you are going to think anyway—you might as well think BIG!" —
Mahatma Gandhi

Month _____   Year _____

My Vision:

_____

_____

_____

_____

_____

_____

My Monthly Goals	Date Achieved
1.	
2.	
3.	
4.	
5.	

People I've Met	Networking Type *(Supporter, Partner, Connector, Mentor, Learner)*
1.	
2.	
3.	
4.	
5.	

Notes/Lessons Learned:

"All our dreams can come true, if we have the courage to pursue them." —
Walt Disney

Month _____   Year _____

My Vision:

_____

_____

_____

_____

_____

_____

My Monthly Goals	*Date Achieved*
1.	
2.	
3.	
4.	
5.	

People I've Met	*Networking Type* *(Supporter, Partner, Connector, Mentor, Learner)*
1.	
2.	
3.	
4.	
5.	

Notes/Lessons Learned:

"Anyone can be average, but can you be superior? Learn to Do Well." —
S. Burns

Month _____   Year _____

My Vision:

_____

_____

_____

_____

_____

_____

My Monthly Goals	Date Achieved
1.	
2.	
3.	
4.	
5.	

| People I've Met | Networking Type |
	(Supporter, Partner, Connector, Mentor, Learner)
1.	
2.	
3.	
4.	
5.	

Notes/Lessons Learned:

Semester Break

Are you still writing in your Vision Planner?

Yes – Great! You are destined to achieve whatever you start.

No – What are you waiting for? This is about you!

"Do, or do not, there is no try." — *Frank Oz*

Month _____   Year _____

My Vision:

_____

_____

_____

_____

_____

_____

My Monthly Goals	Date Achieved
1.	
2.	
3.	
4.	
5.	

People I've Met	Networking Type *(Supporter, Partner, Connector, Mentor, Learner)*
1.	
2.	
3.	
4.	
5.	

Notes/Lessons Learned:

"All know the way, but few actually walk it" — *Bodhidharma*

Month _____   Year _____

My Vision:

_____

_____

_____

_____

_____

_____

My Monthly Goals	Date Achieved
1.	
2.	
3.	
4.	
5.	

People I've Met	Networking Type *(Supporter, Partner, Connector, Mentor, Learner)*
1.	
2.	
3.	
4.	
5.	

Notes/Lessons Learned:

"Dream lofty dreams, and as you dream, so shall you become." —*James Allen*

Month _____   Year _____

My Vision:

_____

_____

_____

_____

_____

_____

My Monthly Goals	*Date Achieved*
1.	
2.	
3.	
4.	
5.	

People I've Met	*Networking Type* *(Supporter, Partner, Connector, Mentor, Learner)*
1.	
2.	
3.	
4.	
5.	

Notes/Lessons Learned:

"Control your destiny or someone else will" — Jack Welch

Month _____   Year _____

My Vision:

_____
_____
_____
_____
_____
_____

My Monthly Goals	Date Achieved
1.	
2.	
3.	
4.	
5.	

People I've Met	Networking Type *(Supporter, Partner, Connector, Mentor, Learner)*
1.	
2.	
3.	
4.	
5.	

Notes/Lessons Learned:

Semester Break

Is Education still a Priority for You?

Yes – Wonderful! No roadblocks will prevent you from achieving your goals.

No – Why not? Only <u>you</u> can answer this question, but you have to be honest with yourself.

"Cherish your vision and your dreams as they are children of your soul; the blueprints of your ultimate achievements." — Napoleon Hill

Month _____   Year _____

My Vision:

_____

_____

_____

_____

_____

_____

My Monthly Goals	*Date Achieved*
1.	
2.	
3.	
4.	
5.	

People I've Met	*Networking Type* *(Supporter, Partner, Connector, Mentor, Learner)*
1.	
2.	
3.	
4.	
5.	

Notes/Lessons Learned:

"Energy and persistence conquer all things." — *Benjamin Franklin*

Month _____   Year _____

My Vision:

_____

_____

_____

_____

_____

_____

My Monthly Goals	Date Achieved
1.	
2.	
3.	
4.	
5.	

People I've met	Networking Type *(Supporter, Partner, Connector, Mentor, Learner)*
1.	
2.	
3.	
4.	
5.	

Notes/Lessons Learned:

"A man's true delight is to do the things he was made for." — Marcus Aurelius

Month ____   Year ____

My Vision:

_____

_____

_____

_____

_____

My Monthly Goals	Date Achieved
1.	
2.	
3.	
4.	
5.	

People I've met	Networking Type (Supporter, Partner, Connector, Mentor, Learner)
1.	
2.	
3.	
4.	
5.	

Notes/Lessons Learned:

"Find something you love to do and you'll never have to work a day in your life." — Harvey Mackay

Month _____   Year _____

My Vision:

_____

_____

_____

_____

_____

_____

My Monthly Goals	Date Achieved
1.	
2.	
3.	
4.	
5.	

People I've met	Networking Type (Supporter, Partner, Connector, Mentor, Learner)
1.	
2.	
3.	
4.	
5.	

Notes/Lessons Learned:

End of the Year Checklist

Review your planner for year 1 and answer the following:

Did your vision change any this year?

☐ Yes   ☐ No

How many goals did you set over the year?

☐ 1 – 12   ☐ 13 - 24   ☐ 25 - 36   ☐ > 37

How many did you accomplish?

☐ 1 – 12   ☐ 13 - 24   ☐ 25 - 36   ☐ > 37

How many of the following networking types did you meet?

Supporters _____   **Connectors** _____

Mentors _____   **Partners** _____

Learners _____

What was your biggest accomplishment this year?

_____

_____

Year 2

Goals (noun) – *something that somebody wants to achieve.* It is difficult to have a vision <u>without</u> having something that you want to achieve. A goal is a target or an aim that will help you to stay on track.

You've made it through year one. Whether you stayed in school, graduated, or took a break, you still made it. Another year is another year to fulfill your purpose.

What did you learn about yourself last year? Even if you don't like what you see in the mirror, you know that seeing is necessary for changing and doing. Are you good at keeping your goals? What goals do you need to retain, and which do you need to modify? Keep in mind that in order to achieve your goals you must be **determined** to achieve them. You can't have a goal of making an A in a class if you don't bother going to class. It simply doesn't work that way.

One way to ensure that you continue meeting your goals is to establish realistic measurable and attainable ones. If you can't measure them, you have no way of knowing if they were truly successful. Only you can decide what is realistic and attainable. Anything is possible, but what must you do to ensure reaching them today? For instance, a student had a goal of international travel, but until the student applied for a passport, international travel was just an unattainable goal.

Keep in mind that you are in control of you…you can dictate and create the when, where, why. Start determining whom you should meet. Do you have too many mentors, but few connectors or partners? Seek to find the right balance of people who will support you during your journey. If you stay on course, you will work through your goals and make the right connections.

If your vision has changed this year, make sure to document those changes in your planner. When determining your monthly goals please note **having one goal and achieving it** is much better than having five goals and not achieving any.

"The tragedy of life doesn't lie in not reaching your goal. The tragedy lies in having no goal to reach." – Benjamin Mays

Month _____   Year _____

My Vision:

_____

_____

_____

_____

_____

_____

My Monthly Goals	*Date Achieved*
1.	
2.	
3.	
4.	
5.	

People I've met	*Networking Type* *(Supporter, Partner, Connector, Mentor, Learner)*
1.	
2.	
3.	
4.	
5.	

Notes/Lessons Learned:

"We aim above the mark to hit the mark." — Ralph Waldo Emerson

Month _____   Year _____

My Vision:

_____

_____

_____

_____

_____

_____

My Monthly Goals	Date Achieved
1.	
2.	
3.	
4.	
5.	

People I've met	Networking Type *(Supporter, Partner ,Connector, Mentor, Learner)*
1.	
2.	
3.	
4.	
5.	

Notes/Lessons Learned:

"First say to yourself what you would be; and then do what you have to do."
— *Epictetus*

Month _____   Year _____

My Vision:

_____

_____

_____

_____

_____

_____

My Monthly Goals	Date Achieved
1.	
2.	
3.	
4.	
5.	

People I've met	Networking Type *(Supporter, Partner ,Connector, Mentor, Learner)*
1.	
2.	
3.	
4.	
5.	

Notes/Lessons Learned:

"If there is a way to do it better...find it." — *Thomas Edison*

Month _____   Year _____

My Vision:

_____

_____

_____

_____

_____

_____

My Monthly Goals	Date Achieved
1.	
2.	
3.	
4.	
5.	

People I've met	Networking Type *(Supporter, Partner, Connector, Mentor, Learner)*
1.	
2.	
3.	
4.	
5.	

Notes/Lessons Learned:

Semester Break

When you look in the mirror, you only see yourself. When you look at your life, the only thing that matters is you. Only you can live it and only you can die by it.

What have you done to make yourself matter?

"Anyone will be unhappy until he recognizes his true calling." —

Month _____   Year _____

My Vision:

_____

_____

_____

_____

_____

_____

My Monthly Goals	*Date Achieved*
1.	
2.	
3.	
4.	
5.	

People I've met	*Networking Type* *(Supporter, Partner, Connector, Mentor, Learner)*
1.	
2.	
3.	
4.	
5.	

Notes/Lessons Learned:

"Everyone thinks of changing the world, but no one thinks of changing himself." — Leo Tolstoy

Month _____   Year _____

My Vision:

_____

_____

_____

_____

_____

_____

My Monthly Goals	*Date Achieved*
1.	
2.	
3.	
4.	
5.	

People I've met	*Networking Type* *(Supporter, Partner ,Connector, Mentor, Learner)*
1.	
2.	
3.	
4.	
5.	

Notes/Lessons Learned:

"If you aim for nothing, you'll hit it every time." — Unknown

Month _____   Year _____

My Vision:

_____

_____

_____

_____

_____

_____

My Monthly Goals	Date Achieved
1.	
2.	
3.	
4.	
5.	

People I've met	Networking Type *(Supporter, Partner, Connector, Mentor, Learner)*
1.	
2.	
3.	
4.	
5.	

Notes/Lessons Learned:

"The greatest thing in this world is not so much where we stand as in what direction we are moving." — *Johann Wolfgang von Goethe*

Month _____   Year _____

My Vision:

_____

_____

_____

_____

_____

_____

My Monthly Goals	Date Achieved
1.	
2.	
3.	
4.	
5.	

People I've met	Networking Type *(Supporter, Partner, Connector, Mentor, Learner)*
1.	
2.	
3.	
4.	
5.	

Notes/Lessons Learned:

Semester Break

If you get to a roadblock, look for a creative way to get around it. For example, if you can't make it to class, try attending the same class at a different time. If transportation becomes an issue, check to see if you can take an online class.

Don't let the roadblock stop you.

"Accept who you are and revel in that." — *Mitch Albom*

Month _____   Year _____

My Vision:

_____

_____

_____

_____

_____

_____

My Monthly Goals	Date Achieved
1.	
2.	
3.	
4.	
5.	

People I've met	Networking Type *(Supporter, Partner, Connector, Mentor, Learner)*
1.	
2.	
3.	
4.	
5.	

Notes/Lessons Learned:

"If you don't know where you're going, you'll probably not wind up there."
— *Forrest Gump*

Month _____   Year _____

My Vision:

_____

_____

_____

_____

_____

_____

My Monthly Goals	Date Achieved
1.	
2.	
3.	
4.	
5.	

| People I've met | Networking Type |
	(Supporter, Partner, Connector, Mentor, Learner)
1.	
2.	
3.	
4.	
5.	

Notes/Lessons Learned:

"It is a funny thing about life: If you refuse to accept anything but the best you very often get it." — *W. Somerset Maugham*

Month _____   Year _____

My Vision:

_____

_____

_____

_____

_____

_____

My Monthly Goals	Date Achieved
1.	
2.	
3.	
4.	
5.	

People I've met	Networking Type *(Supporter, Partner, Connector, Mentor, Learner)*
1.	
2.	
3.	
4.	
5.	

Notes/Lessons Learned:

"When you want something, all the universe conspires in helping you to achieve it." — *Paulo Coelho*

Month _____   Year _____

My Vision:

_____

_____

_____

_____

_____

_____

My Monthly Goals	Date Achieved
1.	
2.	
3.	
4.	
5.	

People I've met	Networking Type *(Supporter, Partner, Connector, Mentor, Learner)*
1.	
2.	
3.	
4.	
5.	

Notes/Lessons Learned:

End of the Year Checklist

Review your planner for year 2 and answer the following:

Did your vision change any this year?

☐ Yes   ☐ No

How many goals did you set over the year?

☐ 1 – 12   ☐ 13 - 24   ☐ 25 - 36   ☐ > 37

How many did you accomplish?

☐ 1 – 12   ☐ 13 - 24   ☐ 25 - 36   ☐ > 37

How many of the following networking types did you meet?

Supporters _____   Connectors _____

Mentors _____   Partners _____

Learners _____

What was your biggest accomplishment this year?

_____

_____

_____

Year 3

Networking (noun) –*gathering of acquaintances or contacts*. Encarta describes networking as "the building up or maintaining of informal relationships, especially with people whose friendship could bring advantages such as job or business opportunities".

The first part of this description is the *building up or maintaining of informal relationships.* Networking requires work, nurturing, and relationships. It is more than just collecting and passing out business cards. Perhaps you talk to your teller at the bank on a regular basis or have something in common with the security guard on your campus. You are relating and developing a relationship. (*Don't be surprised by who those people may know*).

The second part of this description is, *especially with people whose friendship could bring advantages...* The key here is **friendship**. Those who share jobs or business opportunities are most likely your friends (personal, business, church) or those who know your friends. Nurturing relationships to friendships take work, so you must be prepared to make the investment.

In order to get the most out of networking, you should know what you want. People can't assist you if <u>you</u> don't know what you want. Having a vision at this stage is crucial, because networking at this stage is crucial.

Review the networking contacts you have made over the years. How many of those contacts have you actually developed a relationship or friendship? If the answer is "not that many" here's your goal for this year (*please put this on your monthly goal sheet*). Pick up the phone and call them. Invite them to lunch, tell them about your vision and goals for this year, and get to know them. Remember it is not all about them doing for you, but also it's about you being in a position to do for them.

"When you meet anyone, treat the event as a holy encounter." — Wayne Dyer

Month _____   Year _____

My Vision:

_____

_____

_____

_____

_____

_____

My Monthly Goals	Date Achieved
1.	
2.	
3.	
4.	
5.	

People I've met	Networking Type *(Supporter, Partner, Connector, Mentor, Learner)*
1.	
2.	
3.	
4.	
5.	

Notes/Lessons Learned:

"Be the change you want to see in the world." — Mahatma Gandhi

Month _____   Year _____

My Vision:

_____

_____

_____

_____

_____

My Monthly Goals	Date Achieved
1.	
2.	
3.	
4.	
5.	

People I've met	Networking Type (Supporter, Partner, Connector, Mentor, Learner)
1.	
2.	
3.	
4.	
5.	

Notes/Lessons Learned:

"Create each day anew." — *Morihei Ueshiba*

Month _____   Year _____

My Vision:

_____

_____

_____

_____

_____

_____

My Monthly Goals	Date Achieved
1.	
2.	
3.	
4.	
5.	

People I've met	Networking Type (Supporter, Partner, Connector, Mentor, Learner)
1.	
2.	
3.	
4.	
5.	

Notes/Lessons Learned:

"Knowledge is limited. Imagination encircles the world." — *Albert Einstein*

Month _____ Year _____

My Vision:

_____
_____
_____
_____
_____
_____

My Monthly Goals	Date Achieved
1.	
2.	
3.	
4.	
5.	

People I've met	Networking Type
	(Supporter, Partner, Connector, Mentor, Learner))
1.	
2.	
3.	
4.	
5.	

Notes/Lessons Learned:

Semester Break

Why do you have to write your vision every month when it's always the same?

It's a known fact that what you write is what you do…what you become. Therefore, write it until it hurts…until it pushes you to action…to you become what you see.

I'm on top of it – Great! Keep writing it.

I'm guilty, I stopped writing it – Get back to it. It's important.

"Be what is that you are seeking." — *Wayne Dyer*

Month _____   Year _____

My Vision:

_____

_____

_____

_____

_____

_____

My Monthly Goals	Date Achieved
1.	
2.	
3.	
4.	
5.	

People I've met	Networking Type
	(Supporter, Partner, Connector, Mentor, Learner)
1.	
2.	
3.	
4.	
5.	

Notes/Lessons Learned:

"A man's reach should exceed his grasp. Or what's a heaven for?" —
Robert Browning

Month _____   Year _____

My Vision:

_____
_____
_____
_____
_____
_____

My Monthly Goals	Date Achieved
1.	
2.	
3.	
4.	
5.	

People I've met	Networking Type *(Supporter, Partner, Connector, Mentor, Learner)*
1.	
2.	
3.	
4.	
5.	

Notes/Lessons Learned:

"In dreams and in love there are no impossibilities." — *Janos Arany*

Month _____   Year _____

My Vision:

_____

_____

_____

_____

_____

_____

My Monthly Goals	Date Achieved
1.	
2.	
3.	
4.	
5.	

People I've met	Networking Type (Supporter, Partner, Connector, Mentor, Learner)
1.	
2.	
3.	
4.	
5.	

Notes/Lessons Learned:

"If at first you do succeed, try something harder." — *Ann Landers*

Month _____   Year _____

My Vision:

_____

_____

_____

_____

_____

_____

My Monthly Goals	Date Achieved
1.	
2.	
3.	
4.	
5.	

People I've met	Networking Type (Supporter, Partner, Connector, Mentor, Learner)
1.	
2.	
3.	
4.	
5.	

Notes/Lessons Learned:

Semester Break

△

Getting overwhelmed with school, work, life?

Take a mini break. Go get a massage, take a hot bath, or take a long weekend trip. Be kind to yourself – you deserve it!

"A stumbling block to the pessimist is a stepping stone to the optimist."
Eleanor Roosevelt

Month _____   Year _____

My Vision:

_____

_____

_____

_____

_____

_____

My Monthly Goals	Date Achieved
1.	
2.	
3.	
4.	
5.	

People I've met	Networking Type *(Supporter, Partner, Connector, Mentor, Learner)*
1.	
2.	
3.	
4.	
5.	

Notes/Lessons Learned:

"Be occupied, then, with what you really value and let the thief take something else." — *Meviana Rumi*

Month _____   Year _____

My Vision:

_____

_____

_____

_____

_____

_____

My Monthly Goals	Date Achieved
1.	
2.	
3.	
4.	
5.	

People I've met	Networking Type *(Supporter, Partner, Connector, Mentor, Learner)*
1.	
2.	
3.	
4.	
5.	

Notes/Lessons Learned:

"...Your purpose will only be found in service to others and in being connected to the something far greater than your mind/body/ego." — *Wayne Dyer*

Month _____   Year _____

My Vision:

_____

_____

_____

_____

_____

_____

My Monthly Goals	Date Achieved
1.	
2.	
3.	
4.	
5.	

People I've met	Networking Type *(Supporter, Partner, Connector, Mentor, Learner)*
1.	
2.	
3.	
4.	
5.	

Notes/Lessons Learned:

"Continuous effort – not strength or intelligence – is the key to unlocking our potential."– *Winston Churchill*

Month _____   Year _____

My Vision:

_____
_____
_____
_____
_____
_____

My Monthly Goals	Date Achieved
1.	
2.	
3.	
4.	
5.	

People I've met	Networking Type (Supporter, Partner, Connector, Mentor, Learner)
1.	
2.	
3.	
4.	
5.	

Notes/Lessons Learned:

End of the Year Checklist

Review your planner for year 3 and answer the following:

Did your vision change any this year?

☐ Yes   ☐ No

How many goals did you set over the year?

☐ 1 – 12   ☐ 13 - 24   ☐ 25 - 36   ☐ > 37

How many did you accomplish?

☐ 1 – 12   ☐ 13 - 24   ☐ 25 - 36   ☐ > 37

How many of the following networking types did you meet?

Supporters _____   Connectors _____

Mentors   _____   Partners   _____

Learners   _____

What was your biggest accomplishment this year?

_____

_____

Year 4

Evolve (verb) *–to develop something gradually, often into something more complex or advanced, or undergo such development.* This year is about evolving…growing. You may feel like you have grown tremendously in three years but this year will bring forth a greater evolution.

If you have worked this planner since month one, year one, congratulations! You have committed yourself to improving yourself! Please understand that during this year, things will begin to evolve, and your vision will have more focus. Do not become fearful as your vision comes closer. Remember the intro: An unclear vision can lead to sickness, so just know that you have been working very hard to accomplish your goals, and you can't break down now.

You too, are evolving…becoming more aware of your identity and the vision you want. The person that you have evolved into is the person who will carry you through this year. Embrace growth and seek to do new things this year.

If your vision is to graduate and this is your graduation year, create a new vision now. Remember: a vision is what you want to become – something that you are not now. Dig deeper and desire more for yourself!

If you haven't developed a vision yet, STOP! Go no further. Why continue down this path? (*This does not apply to the person who is just using this planner for taking notes☺.*) Where are your goals leading you? If you have all the money in the world, what would you want to do with your life? The answer may lead you to your purpose.

Have a great Year 4 and strive for your destiny!

"Destiny is not a matter of chance, but of choice. Not something to wish for, but to attain." — *William Jennings Bryan*

Month _____   Year _____

My Vision:

_____

_____

_____

_____

_____

_____

My Monthly Goals	Date Achieved
1.	
2.	
3.	
4.	
5.	

People I've Met	Networking Type *(Supporter, Partner, Connector, Mentor, Learner)*
1.	
2.	
3.	
4.	
5.	

Notes/Lessons Learned:

"Don't measure yourself by what you have accomplished, but by what you should have accomplished with your ability. — John Wooden

Month _____   Year _____

My Vision:

_____
_____
_____
_____
_____
_____

My Monthly Goals	Date Achieved
1.	
2.	
3.	
4.	
5.	

People I've Met	Networking Type (Supporter, Partner, Connector, Mentor, Learner)
1.	
2.	
3.	
4.	
5.	

Notes/Lessons Learned:

"A winner is someone who recognizes his God-given talents, works his tail off to develop them into skills and uses these skills to accomplish his goals."— Larry Bird

Month _____   Year _____

My Vision:

_____

_____

_____

_____

_____

_____

My Monthly Goals	Date Achieved
1.	
2.	
3.	
4.	
5.	

People I've Met	Networking Type *(Supporter, Partner, Connector, Mentor, Learner)*
1.	
2.	
3.	
4.	
5.	

Notes/Lessons Learned:

"Never confuse motion with action." — Benjamin Franklin

Month _____   Year _____

My Vision:

_____

_____

_____

_____

_____

_____

My Monthly Goals	*Date Achieved*
1.	
2.	
3.	
4.	
5.	

People I've Met	*Networking Type* *(Supporter, Partner, Connector, Mentor, Learner)*
1.	
2.	
3.	
4.	
5.	

Notes/Lessons Learned:

Semester Break

Make <u>this</u> year count – Do something that will have an impact!

How would you like to be remembered this year? What legacy will you leave? Now is the time to think about it.

Month _____   Year _____

My Vision:

_____

_____

_____

_____

_____

_____

My Monthly Goals	*Date Achieved*
1.	
2.	
3.	
4.	
5.	

People I've Met	*Networking Type* *(Supporter, Partner, Connector, Mentor, Learner)*
1.	
2.	
3.	
4.	
5.	

Notes/Lessons Learned:

"It doesn't matter how one was brought up. What determines the way one does anything is personal power."– Carlos Castaneda

Month _____   Year _____

My Vision:

_____

_____

_____

_____

_____

_____

My Monthly Goals	Date Achieved
1.	
2.	
3.	
4.	
5.	

People I've Met	Networking Type (Supporter, Partner, Connector, Mentor, Learner)
1.	
2.	
3.	
4.	
5.	

Notes/Lessons Learned:

"I do not like to repeat successes. I like to go on to other things." — *Walt Disney*

Month _____   Year _____

My Vision:

_____

_____

_____

_____

_____

_____

My Monthly Goals	Date Achieved
1.	
2.	
3.	
4.	
5.	

People I've Met	Networking Type *(Supporter, Partner, Connector, Mentor, Learner)*
1.	
2.	
3.	
4.	
5.	

Notes/Lessons Learned:

"The sign of a great man is that the closer you get, the greater he seems." — *Chofetz Chaim*

Month _____   Year _____

My Vision:

_____
_____
_____
_____
_____
_____

My Monthly Goals	*Date Achieved*
1.	
2.	
3.	
4.	
5.	

People I've Met	*Networking Type* *(Supporter, Partner, Connector, Mentor, Learner)*
1.	
2.	
3.	
4.	
5.	

Notes/Lessons Learned:

Semester Break

Invest in yourself

Making an investment in yourself means you don't just simply go to class or go to work—you invest in it. You do more than just show up. You bring ideas, collaboration, and leadership to the table. Do more than just meet expectations—exceed them!

"Outstanding people have one thing in common: an absolute sense of mission." — *Zig Zigler*

Month _____   Year _____

My Vision:

_____

_____

_____

_____

_____

_____

My Monthly Goals	*Date Achieved*
1.	
2.	
3.	
4.	
5.	

People I've Met	*Networking Type* *(Supporter, Partner, Connector, Mentor, Learner)*
1.	
2.	
3.	
4.	
5.	

Notes/Lessons Learned:

"The kingdom of God is within you." — *Jesus*

Month _____   Year _____

My Vision:

_____

_____

_____

_____

_____

_____

My Monthly Goals	*Date Achieved*
1.	
2.	
3.	
4.	
5.	

People I've Met	*Networking Type* *(Supporter, Partner, Connector, Mentor, Learner)*
1.	
2.	
3.	
4.	
5.	

Notes/Lessons Learned:

"Here is a test to find out whether your mission in life is complete. If you're alive, it isn't."– Richard Bach

Month _____   Year _____

My Vision:

_____

_____

_____

_____

_____

_____

My Monthly Goals	*Date Achieved*
1.	
2.	
3.	
4.	
5.	

People I've Met	*Networking Type* *(Supporter, Partner, Connector, Mentor, Learner)*
1.	
2.	
3.	
4.	
5.	

Notes/Lessons Learned:

"Make the impossible possible." - Unknown

Month _____   Year _____

My Vision:

_____

_____

_____

_____

_____

_____

My Monthly Goals	*Date Achieved*
1.	
2.	
3.	
4.	
5.	

People I've Met	*Networking Type* *(Supporter, Partner, Connector, Mentor, Learner)*
1.	
2.	
3.	
4.	
5.	

Notes/Lessons Learned:

End of the Year Checklist

Review your planner for year 4 and answer the following:

Did your vision change any this year?

☐   Yes   ☐   No

How many goals did you set over the year?

☐   1 – 12   ☐   13 - 24   ☐   25 - 36   ☐   > 37

How many did you accomplish?

☐   1 – 12   ☐   13 - 24   ☐   25 - 36   ☐   > 37

How many of the following networking types did you meet?

Supporters _____   **Connectors** _____

Mentors _____   **Partners** _____

Learners _____

What was your biggest accomplishment this year?

_____

_____

Final Thoughts

Action (noun) *–the process of doing something in order to achieve a purpose.* Well, you did it. Four years of developing a vision, creating goals, and networking! Reflect on your four year journey. What do you see? How have you grown? What has made you most proud?

The next stage of your journey is about **action**. You have to work the networks, work the goals, and work the vision. You have to take everything you have learned so far and put it to action.

Don't forget to thank those who have helped you get this far…those who have invested their time and money. Also, make sure you impart your knowledge to others. Offer a support to someone else who is just getting started. If this vision planner has helped you, recommend it to someone else!

Going forward, I believe that you will have new ideas, new thoughts, and new visions…Visions that will lead you to a larger vision. Decide what you want to experience in your life, and experience it. No one will ever stop you but you. *You create your own destiny!*

Remember, learning never stops: Only your desire to do so. So continue to move forth, learn as much as you can, and be kind to yourself.

God Bless!

Stephanie R. Burns

Next Step:
Vision Planner – Professional Edition

www.ingramcontent.com/pod-product-compliance
Lightning Source LLC
Chambersburg PA
CBHW030024290326
41934CB00005B/475